THE G.I. SERIES

Marines
in Vietnam

Corporal Peter Behrens, and his dog Mark, from the 1st Light Anti-Aircraft Missile (LAAM) battalion, guard one of their battalion's Hawk missile launchers outside Da Nang airport. The 1st LAAM were deployed to Vietnam in February 1965 after Communist attacks on the nearby airfield. Although it had not yet begun to be general issue to Marines at this point, Behrens has been able to obtain a set of the 1st Pattern tropical combat uniform. (U.S.M.C.)

THE G.I. SERIES

THE ILLUSTRATED HISTORY OF THE AMERICAN SOLDIER, HIS UNIFORM AND HIS EQUIPMENT

Marines in Vietnam

Christopher J. Anderson

Pen & Sword
MILITARY

Marines in Vietnam

A Greenhill Book
First published in 2002 by Greenhill Books,
Lionel Leventhal Limited
www.greenhillbooks.com

This edition published in 2016 by
PEN & SWORD MILITARY
An imprint of
Pen & Sword Books Ltd
47 Church Street
Barnsley,
South Yorkshire
S70 2AS

Copyright © Lionel Leventhal Limited, 2002

ISBN: 978-1-84832-810-5

CIP data records for this title are available from the
British Library

Designed by DAG Publications Ltd
Design by David Gibbons
Layout by Anthony A. Evans

Printed and bound in Malta by Gutenberg Press Ltd

Pen & Sword Books Ltd incorporates the Imprints
of Aviation, Atlas, Family History, Fiction, Maritime,
Military, Discovery, Politics, History, Archaeology,
Select, Wharncliffe Local History, Wharncliffe True
Crime, Military Classics, Wharncliffe Transport,
Leo Cooper, The Praetorian Press, Remember When,
Seaforth Publishing and Frontline Publishing.

For a complete list of Pen & Sword titles
please contact
PEN & SWORD BOOKS LIMITED
47 Church Street, Barnsley, South Yorkshire,
S70 2AS, England
E-mail: enquiries@pen-and-sword.co.uk
Website: www.pen-and-sword.co.uk

PICTURE CREDITS
NA   National Archives, Washington, DC
U.S.M.C.   United States Marine Corps

MARINES IN VIETNAM

On the morning of March 8, 1965, as tens of thousands of their predecessors had done countless times before during the renowned history of the United States Marine Corps, the 1,400 young men of the 9th Marine Expeditionary Brigade (MEB) made final preparations to their equipment while waiting for the order to board their landing craft and head toward the beach. Finally, everything was in order and the Marines boarded their landing craft and headed toward Red Beach II, which was just a little over a mile away from the air base at Da Nang in the Republic of Vietnam (RVN).

What they found when their landing craft ground ashore at 9.30 in the morning, however, was not a heavily defended beach bristling with enemy fortifications, but scores of beautiful young Vietnamese girls who were soon draping flowers on the battle-ready, but startled, Marines. It was an awkward introduction to what would become a long and very confusing war. Before the last man left in April 1975, more than half a million Marines served in Vietnam. Although the Marines of the 9th MEB could not possibly have imagined it at the time, they were in the vanguard of what would become the longest war in the Corps' history.

The men of Brig. Gen. Frederick Karch's 9th MEB had been deployed in response to North Vietnamese attacks on the vital air base at Da Nang, where the Marine's 362nd Medium Helicopter Battalion had been operating in support of RVN forces since 1962. As the tempo of Communist attacks against American positions intensified during late 1964 and early 1965, the decision had been made to send the 1st Light Anti-Aircraft Missile Battalion to assist in the defense of the airbase. Da Nang airbase was located in the I Corps Tactical Zone (the Republic of Vietnam was divided into four tactical zones) and was the northernmost zone of operations in the Republic of Vietnam. The Corps' northern border was defined by the demilitarized zone (DMZ) that separated North and South Vietnam from one another.

Despite the addition of the missile battalion to Da Nang's defenses, General William C. Westmoreland, the commander of the U.S. Military Assistance Command, Vietnam (MACV), believed that he required additional U.S. troops if he was going to be able to defend U.S.

installations in South Vietnam and in February the decision was made to send the 9th MEB to reinforce those Marines already at Da Nang. The assignment of Karch's Marines to the defense of Da Nang airfield meant that I Corps would become the Marine Corp's home during its time in Vietnam and the focus of the majority of its operations.

Although they had arrived ready to enter combat (while one battalion landed at Red Beach, another battalion had been airlifted directly to Da Nang), Karch's men were restricted to maintaining defensive positions around the airfield and, initially, were not allowed to go into the interior of the country in pursuit of Communist units. The sole job of the Marines was perimeter defense of the airfield.

In many respects it was probably just as well. Karche's men needed time to adjust to their new surroundings and improve the airfield's facilities. No real attempt had been made to equip the men who landed at Red Beach II with the clothing and equipment suitable for operations in Vietnam. The men of the 9th MEB landed wearing the heavy Army issue OG107, cotton sateen utility uniform and heavy black leather combat boots. Their M1961 load-carrying equipment (LCE) consisted of a pistol belt and ammunition pouches supported by World War II-era combat suspenders and the Marines' ubiquitous 782 Gear. First introduced in 1941, the 782 Gear included a haversack and knapsack, both with a tiny carrying capacity.

For the first several months in Vietnam, as North Vietnamese harassing attacks continued and more and more men and equipment arrived, the Marines around Da Nang became more accustomed to their surroundings and carried out short patrols. By April, with President Lyndon B. Johnson's decision to send additional U.S. forces to Vietnam, authority was granted for the Marines to make longer patrols into the interior. On April 22, 1965, one of these patrols had the Marines, first sustained encounter with a Viet Cong (VC) unit.

By May, additional Marine units had established another base at Chu Lai and, reflecting the increased level of commitment in I Corps, on May 6, the 9th MEB was designated the III Marine Expeditionary Force (MEF) and the 3rd Marine Division moved its headquarters from Okinawa, Japan, to Vietnam. On June 3, Maj. Gen.

Lewis Walt was appointed to command the III MAF and he was soon occupied in developing the means of coming to grips with Communist forces in his area.

One of the ways of combatting the enemy forces that was quickly hit upon was to become involved in a wide variety of programs with the local population. Many of these programs were not specifically military and were intended to win the Vietnamese villagers 'hearts and minds.' The most successful involved the deployment of Combined Action Program (CAP) platoons. CAP platoons would live in Vietnamese villages among the people, helping to defend the villages and training local militia units in self-defense. As General Walt observed soon after taking command, 'We are in the pacification business.' Throughout their time in Vietnam, and often times over the objection of Westmoreland and other Army officials, Marines would encourage close interaction with and assistance to the local Vietnamese population; measures which today are considered among the most successful American initiatives of the war.

Striking back at an increasingly difficult enemy, however, was also at the forefront of Walt's thinking. Although the Marines, area of responsibility around Da Nang had been slowly expanding, it was not until July that Walt was finally given the authority to aggressively pursue enemy formations. On August 16, acting on information that the 1st VC Regiment was located in the Van Tuong Peninsula, just 15 miles from the Marine base at Chu Lai, Walt launched Operation Starlight. The operation involved Marine and Army of the Republic of Vietnam (ARVN) air and ground forces in a large-scale operation. The action was successful and over the course of the next six days Walt's men killed almost a thousand enemy soldiers and crippled the 1st VC Regiment. In addition to the destruction of the enemy regiment, the operation gave the Marines confidence that they could come to grips with and defeat their enemy.

Following Operation Starlight, the remainder of 1965 was spent on continuing the buildup of U.S. forces in I Corps, expanding pacification efforts within the Corps' provinces and, in December the joint Marine, ARVN operation, Harvest Moon. Launched in December, Harvest Moon was intended to destroy a resurgent 1st VC Regiment around the provincial capitals of Hiep Duc and Que Son. Although ARVN forces performed poorly, by the time the operation ended on December 20, the Marines claimed to have killed more than 400 Viet Cong soldiers and again severely damaged the 1st VC Regiment. Although slow to start, by the end of 1965, the Marines had conducted 15 large-scale operations against an enemy they were becoming more and more familiar with.

The first few months of 1966 saw increasing numbers of Marines arriving in Vietnam, and by March the 3rd Marine Division was joined by the 1st. With this additional manpower, Walt was able to expand his pacification efforts while at the same time launching larger operations against North Vietnamese Army units operating along the DMZ. While the 3rd Division would engage North Vietnamese units in the north, the 1st Division would be busy with pacification efforts and in dealing with VC units in I Corps' interior. Unfortunately, while Walt hoped to expand his pacification efforts, much of his attention was focused on a revolt of ARVN units in I Corps during the first part of the year. Nevertheless, a series of operations was carried out against NVA units operating against bases in the northern and western portions of I Corps. Operations Double Eagle, New York, Utah and Texas all involved substantial Marine assets.

However, the largest operation of that year, and the largest operation of the war up to that point, was Hastings, which began on July 15. The operation was intended to stop North Vietnam's 324B Division, which had crossed the DMZ into South Vietnam in Quang Tin province, from advancing any further. Initially, three Marine battalions were deployed to check the advance and before long this force was joined by three additional U.S. battalions and five ARVN battalions. Fighting was fierce, and on July 28, elements of the 4th Marines defeated 1000-man human-wave assaults reminiscent of some of the worst fighting in the Pacific during World War II. Although the North Vietnamese were eventually forced to retreat, they soon returned to the area. The subsequent fight, known as Operation Prairie, would continue into the following year.

The Marines' first full year in Vietnam had seen a dramatic increase in the size of their commitment, as well as the tempo of the fighting. As the III MAF found itself more familiar with its new battleground, it became more aggressive in going after North Vietnamese units and in expanding its pacification efforts within I Corps.

Responding to the nature of the fighting, the appearance of the Marines was slowly beginning to change. By the end of 1966, Marine units began receiving sets of the 1st Pattern Tropical Combat Uniform, the famous "jungle" uniform. Made of lightweight cotton poplin, the jungle uniform, which had been inspired by the famous M1942 paratrooper uniform of World War II, was lighter in weight than the utility uniform and featured bellows pockets on jacket and trousers that had far greater carrying capacity. Interestingly, unlike previous utility uniforms, the jungle jacket was not issued with the Marines' beloved Eagle, Globe and Anchor (EGA) insignia stenciled to the left breast. Although not official, Marines in I Corps also began to acquire and use a wide variety of Army equipment. As soon as they were able, most Marines would obtain sets of Army issue M1956 LCE. Much had changed since the first Marines had come ashore in March 1965 and by the end of 1966, there were more than 70,000 Marines in Vietnam.

The first few months of 1967 saw a continuation of Operation Prairie and fighting along the DMZ and around Khe Sanh. The battles around the special forces base at Khe Sanh soon came to be known among the Marines as the 'hill fights.' The battles for Hills 558, 861 and 881 North and South were particularly brutal as

Marines fought in wet and cold conditions to force North Vietnamese units from well-prepared positions. In addition, fierce fighting was encountered around the Marine base at Con Thien, just two miles south of the DMZ and a part of the 'McNamara Line.' The McNamara line featured a series of listening devices stretched along the length of the DMZ intended to impede enemy infiltration into South Vietnam. The fighting around Con Thien, which many dubbed a 'siege,' continued through October and earned from the Marines who fought there the sobriquet 'the Meat Grinder,' for the terrible toll it took of American lives.

The third year in Vietnam had been significant in a number of ways. The fighting continued in intensity along the DMZ and Westmoreland began to focus increased attention on the Marine base at Khe Sanh. In June, Lt. Gen. Robert E. Cushman replaced Walt, and improved weapons and equipment began to reach the units in the field. During the hill fights in May, the venerable M14 rifle began to be replaced by the new M16 rifle, the ANPRC/10 radio began to be replaced by the more effective ANPRC/25 and improvements were made to the Marines M1955 flak vest. Marines operating in the jungle were now, by and large, all equipped with the new utility uniform. However, perhaps the most sobering milestone of 1967 was that by the end of the year, Marine casualties surpassed those suffered in Korea. What had begun as a limited deployment of a perimeter security force had become the second costliest war in Marine Corps history.

As the war escalated and more and more soldiers began to arrive in Vietnam, Westmoreland was able to send additional Army units to strengthen the U.S. position in I Corps. The arrival of Army units freed the Marines of some of their responsibilities and the 1st Marine Division was able to transfer to Thua Thien province and the 3rd Marine Division was allowed to concentrate in Quang Tri province. The Marine's two principal formations in Vietnam were now concentrated in the two northernmost provinces of the Republic of Vietnam where, early in 1968, they would see some of the most intense fighting of the entire war.

For the 3rd Division, much of that fighting would be conducted around the combat base of Khe Sanh. Although it had been established as just one of several bases just south of the DMZ, it took on increased importance as more and more North Vietnamese units surrounded and attempted to destroy it. Westmoreland saw the NVA buildup around the base as an opportunity to inflict serious casualties on his opponent. On January 20, elements of three North Vietnamese divisions attacked the positions of the 26th Marines and their supporting elements. Although their attack seized many perimeter positions, Khe Sanh held. With North Vietnamese units now well placed in the hills surrounding the base, the garrison settled in for a siege. Although the fighting was often fierce, the Marines never feared that the base would be taken. From the beginning, reliance was placed on massive amounts of aerial support. Throughout January and February, as C-130 cargo aircraft braved North Vietnamese anti-aircraft fire to supply the garrison, Air Force and Marine fighter-bombers launched more than 24,000 sorties against NVA positions in what was dubbed Operation Niagra. In addition, the fighter-bombers' attacks were complimented by 2,700 B-52 bomber strikes. The siege continued until April, when Marine and Army units linked up. With its usefulness past, Khe Sanh was dismantled in June.

Meanwhile, as the struggle continued at Khe Sanh and the areas surrounding it, the 1st Division found itself engaged in an equally fierce contest around the ancient city of Hue. Although they had announced a truce from January 27 to February 3 in honor of the Tet New Year celebrations, the North Vietnamese launched a massive offensive throughout South Vietnam. At 3.30 in the morning of January 31, Communist forces seized control of the city of Hue, the ancient capital of Vietnam. Moving quickly against startled ARVN units, the Communists quickly gained control of the city. Fighting in an urban environment rather than the usual hills and jungles, elements of the 1st and 5th Marines, along with RVN army and marine units, were soon fighting to retake the city. Gaining the upper hand in a series of brutal house-to-house encounters, Marine and RVN units were able to regain control of much of the city over the course of the next ten days. Operations would continue through February and the battle would be officially declared over on March 2. The cost, however, had been heavy. It was later estimated that the U.S. Marines suffered a casualty for every yard of ground they retook during the battle.

Although there were frequent pitched battles with North Vietnamese troops, most noticeably in May when elements of the 3rd Marine Division were heavily engaged near Dong Ha, the defeat of the Communist Tet Offensive had dealt a severe blow to Communist forces and the intensity of their attacks began to taper off. During the course of the fighting, Marine strength in Vietnam had peaked at 85,000 and everywhere, it seemed, Marine units had been able to inflict crippling blows on their North Vietnamese opponents.

Reflecting further evolution in uniforms and equipment more suitable to their area of operations, after the Tet Offensive, Marines began to receive ERDL (Engineer Research and Development Laboratories) camouflage uniforms. Originally intended for reconnaissance units, by the end of the year the camouflage jungle uniform was being received in quantity by ordinary Marine units.

1968 had been a pivotal year. Despite the overwhelming defeat of their Tet offensive, the North Vietnamese were able to win the war of popular opinion and as anti-war protests in the United States continued, President Lyndon Johnston announced in May that he would begin to de-escalate the war. In July General Creighton Abrahms replaced Westmoreland as commander of MACV and in November President-elect Richard M. Nixon announced that upon assuming office he would begin the withdrawal of U.S. forces.

Even with the changing political situation, however, fighting in I Corps continued. On January 22, in an operation more reminiscent of those carried out by the Army's air assault divisions, the 9th Marines launched Operation Dewey Canyon into the Song Da Krong Valley in the southwestern corner of Quang Tri province. The operation, which saw the Marines finally able to pursue enemy formations into Laos for the first time, lasted into March and accounted for more than 1,600 enemy dead and huge caches of weapons and supplies captured. The operation was later called, 'the most successful regimental level action of the war.' Although they could not have known it, Dewey Canyon also marked the last large-scale Marine operation of the war. Significant changes were about to begin within the III MAF.

On March 26, Lt. Gen. Herman Nickerson replaced General Cushman as III MAF commander and for the first time, large numbers of Marines began to leave Vietnam as part of President Nixon's plan to have the South Vietnamese bear a greater amount of the burden of conducting the war. The first Marines to leave were from the 9th, which began to leave in August following the successful completion of Dewey Canyon. Withdrawal continued through the fall as the remainder of the 3rd Division continued to engage enemy formations in the Que Son Mountains, and the 1st was engaged in the rice paddies of Quang Nam province. By September, the 3rd Marine Division had completed its redeployment to Okinawa, and by the end of the year Marine strength had been reduced to 55,000 men.

With America's military involvement rapidly diminishing and with the increased emphasis on 'Vietnamization,' a good deal of effort during 1970 was placed on programs such as CAP. The III MAF's area of responsibility was reduced to Quang Nam province and, for the first time since 1965, the Army became the predominant service in I Corps. On March 9, when the headquarters of the III MAF was moved to a smaller facility at Red Beach, Lt. Gen. Keith McCutcheon replaced General Nickerson. McCutcheon only served a short time and was replaced by Lt. Gen. Donn Robertson in December.

While still working on pacification efforts in Quang Nam, McCutcheon, and then Robertson, was also busy handling the withdrawal of additional Marine elements. By May 1971, Marine strength in Vietnam had been reduced to less than 42,000 and the departure of additional units from I Corps continued throughout 1971. On April 9, the III MAF launched its last mission in Vietnam. Operation Scott Orchard was launched into a suspected POW compound and the four-day operation resulted in four NVA casualties and no Marine losses. Six days later, the III MAF returned to Okinawa and the 3d Marine Amphibious Brigade (MAB), with 15,000 Marines were all that remained. The 3d MAB continued operations until May 7 and it was deactivated on June 27, 1971. By December of that year, only 500 Marines remained in South Vietnam where they served as embassy guards and in a variety of administrative roles.

From 1972–1975, as more and more American combat forces were withdrawn (the last American ground forces had departed by August 1972), South Vietnamese forces (backed by massive amounts of U.S. airpower) fought to keep the North Vietnamese from winning control of their country. In response to the North Vietnamese Easter Offensive in 1972, two Marine air groups returned to South Vietnam to provide air support but no Marine ground forces were committed. Following the Paris Peace Accord of January 1973, a tenuous truce existed between the two Vietnam until December 1974 when the North Vietnamese launched their final offensive into the South.

Communist forces were successful everywhere, and as the North Vietnamese offensive picked up steam it became increasingly clear that the South Vietnamese would be unable to stop them. On April 29, 1975, President Gerald R. Ford ordered the Marines to commence Operation Frequent Wind, the evacuation of remaining U.S. personnel from Saigon.

For the next two days, as Communist forces streamed victoriously into Saigon, two heavy helicopter squadrons, HMH-462 and HMH-463, and a battalion landing team of the 4th Marines under the command of Brigadier General Richard Carey, evacuated the last American personnel from Vietnam. The final helicopter lifted off from the roof of the U.S. embassy in Saigon at 7.53 a.m. as desperate South Vietnamese civilians swarmed into the compound. It was the last act of the Vietnam War.

Vietnam had been the Marines' longest conflict and 730,000 men and women had served between 1965–1975. By way of comparison, total enrollment in the Marine Corps during World War II had been 600,000. The Corps' ten-year involvement in South-East Asia was also its second costliest war. During the countless numbers of pitched battles, ambushes and skirmishes throughout I Corps, 19,733 Marines had been killed in action and an additional 67,207 were wounded. Marines accounted for a third of all U.S. casualties suffered during the Vietnam War.

FOR FURTHER READING

Simmons, Edwin, *Marines: The Illustrated History of the Vietnam War*. Bantam Books, 1987.

Murphy, Edward, *Semper FI Vietnam: From Da Nang to the DMZ, Marine Corps Campaigns, 1965–1975*. Presidio Press, 1997.

Summers, Harry, *Historical Atlas of the Vietnam War*. Houghton Mifflin, 1995.

Stanton, Shelby, *Vietnam Order of Battle*. Galahad Books, 1986.

Lyles, Kevin, *Vietnam: U.S. Uniforms in Color Photographs*. Windrow and Greene, 1992.

Above: A 3rd Marine Division M60 machine-gunner fires on enemy positions during a firefight in 1965. The 23-lb M60 served as the rifle squad's automatic weapon and was crucial in combat. The gun could spew up to 100 rounds of 7.62-mm ammunition per minute at the enemy. To the gunner's left is his assistant, armed with an M14 rifle. (U.S.M.C.)

Below: Two members of the 1st Battalion, 5th Marines, try to locate a sniper during an action in November 1967. The Marine in the foreground has attached a rubber-retaining band around his helmet cover. Unlike the Army, which issued an elasticized band for use on the M1, Marines would frequently improvise such devices by cutting up old inner tubes. (U.S.M.C.)

Left: A member of the 3rd Reconnaissance Battalion disembarks from a helicopter at the start of an operation in February 1967. The black stripes on his uniform might be one of the many tiger-stripe camo patterns available in Vietnam and favored by elite units. He is wearing a locally manufactured boonie hat. To protect his hands he wears Army M1950 black leather gloves. He has removed the finger of his glove that would normally cover his trigger finger. (U.S.M.C.)

Below: Troops of the 1st Battalion, 3rd Marines, cross a swiftly moving stream during Operation Newton in November 1967. In addition to his other equipment, the man at the front is carrying a PRC-10 radio. As was frequently done in Vietnam, he has wrapped the mouthpiece for his radio's handset in a plastic bag (visible on his left shoulder) to protect it from moisture and humidity. (U.S.M.C.)

Above: A Marine M-67 'flame tank' (a variant of the M-48 tank equipped with a flame-thrower) sprays enemy positions with napalm during an operation in 1968. Although it is dirty from use, the Marine's peculiar shade of green paint for its vehicles and much of its equipment is visible on this tank. The vehicle commander is wearing the Army issue Combat Vehicle Crewman's (CVC) helmet. Both the Army and Marine Corps used the CVC. (U.S.M.C.)

Right: During the siege at Khe Sanh, L.Cpl. R. L. Fester (left), PFC E. Robertson (center) and PFC R. J. Schere fire their 81-mm mortar on enemy positions. The 132lb 81mm mortar could reach targets up to 3,800 yards away. Although it was heavy, in fixed positions the 81 mm could provide much needed additional firepower. (NA)

Above: PFC Hundall (left) and PFC Smith (right) work to improve their position at Khe Sanh. The presence of North Vietnamese troops in the hills surrounding the base meant that Marines spent much of their time working on World War I-type positions. Smith is using an M1951 combination tool to dig his position while Hundall holds onto one of the thousands of green nylon sandbags that were flown into Khe Sanh to build defensive positions. (NA)

Left: Marines wait in a shallow trench for the C-123 aircraft that will take them away from Khe Sanh in February 1968. With the ever-present threat of enemy mortar fire, they are all wearing M1955 flak jackets and M1 helmets over their tropical combat uniforms. The photograph also shows the popular leather and nylon tropical combat 'jungle' boot, which replaced the earlier black leather combat boot. (U.S.M.C.)

Right: Members of the 2nd Battalion, 3rd Marines, prepare to take a UH-1E Huey helicopter off Mutter's Ridge during Operation Lancaster II. The Huey was the workhorse of both Army and Marine helicopter units during the war. (U.S.M.C.)

Centre right: PFC James Jones from the 2nd Battalion, 5th Marines, helps a Vietnamese child to safety during the fighting for Hue. Rather than wear a helmet, Jones is wearing the distinctive Marine Corps Utility Cap. This cap, which had its origins during World War II, was unique to the Corps and prized by Marines. On the front of the cover (the Marine term for all headgear) a black decal of the Marine's eagle, globe and anchor insignia would be applied. (NA).

Bottom right: A Marine M60 team fire their gun at enemy positions. The weight of the weapon, and its tremendous rate of fire, meant that M60 gunners would normally have an assistant who would carry additional ammunition and assist in the gun's operation. While the assistant wears the cotton M1941 haversack, the gunner has been able to obtain a larger ARVN rucksack. The M1941 haversack, part of the M1941 pack system, was originally developed during World War II. The pack system was universally known among Marines as 782 Gear. (U.S.M.C.)

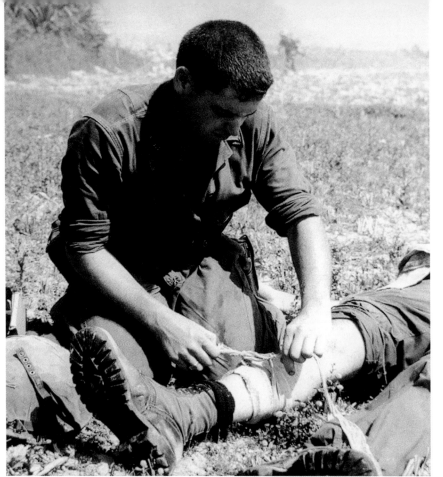

Left: A Navy corpsman bandages a wounded Marine. Unlike the Army, which had its own medical corps, the Marine Corps relied on the Navy, its parent service, to provide medical personnel to its troops in the field. Navy medics were uniformed and equipped in the same way as the Marines they served. The Corpsman is armed: he carries a Colt .45 Auto in its black leather holster. The cleated sole on the wounded man's jungle boots is clearly visible in the picture. Army issue black socks can be seen over the top of the boots. (NA)

Below: A UH-34 helicopter drops men of the 1st Marine Division off at the start of an operation. Marines were instructed to get away from a helicopter as soon as possible after landing. If the landing zone was 'hot' the presence of helicopters would quickly draw enemy fire. First introduced in 1955, the older UH-34 was seen as frequently among Marine units as the UH-1 Huey was seen by Army units. (U.S.M.C.)

Right: Marines of the 1st Marine Division use a Husky to traverse a rice paddy during an operation in September 1969. The Marine at left is wearing a pair of camouflage trousers. The Marines began to issue the camouflage jungle uniform, known officially as: Coat/ Trousers, Man's, Camouflage Cotton, Wind Resistant Poplin, Class 2, to all its personnel during the final months of 1968. The camouflage pattern was referred to as ERDL, an acronym for the Army's Engineer Research and Development Laboratories. (U.S.M.C.)

Below: Marine "grunts" from the 2nd Battalion, 5th Marines, climb Hill 825 during a combat patrol in August 1969. These heavily laden Marines illustrate the typical appearance of Marine riflemen in the field. The marine at the center of the column is wearing a pair of ERDL camouflage trousers. To make himself as comfortable as possible, he has chosen to wear his flak jacket without a jacket or T-shirt; his comrades all appear to wear their flak jackets over T-shirts. (U.S.M.C.)

Above: Corporal George M. Ishihara (left) mans his .50-caliber machinegun as his M-48 tank prepares to move. Note the improvised pintle for the vehicle's .50 MG on top of the cupola turret intended for it. It was found that this external arrangement - despite exposing the gunman - enabled a more effective field of fire. Both of the vehicle crewmen are wearing the nylon CVC helmet, which featured an internal headset and hands-free microphone. While Ishihara wears a set of ERDL camouflage, his companion wears a T-shirt underneath his flak vest. (U.S.M.C.)

Left: An A-4 Skyhawk strike fighter from VMA-311 prepares to take off on the unit's 10,000th combat sortie. Marines operating within I Corps relied heavily on Marine aviation to provide air support during operations. The ground crewmen on the left and right are wearing the Army OG107 utility uniform; the man on the right is wearing the Marine's distinctive utility cap. The pilot is wearing Navy issue flight coveralls and helmet. (NA)

Right: Marines from the 3rd Battalion, 4th Marine Regiment, cross a stream during a sweep and clear mission in Hue-Phu Bai district in July 1964. These men are all wearing Army OG 107 utility uniforms with the Marine Corps' distinctive utility cover. The man in the foreground has an M1941 haversack strapped to his back. Rather than carry his entrenching tool on the back of his pack, this man has decided to clip an extra canteen to the two eyelets on the back of his pack. (U.S.M.C.)

Below: Ontos of the 3rd Marine Division come ashore at Chu Li in Quang Tin Province in May 1965. In Vietnam the Ontos (which is Greek for 'the thing') was unique to the Marines. Originally designed as an antitank weapon, in Vietnam the Ontos, 6-106-mm recoilless rifles were ideal for infantry support. (U.S.M.C.)

Left: A UH-34 lands atop the 'Rockpile' during an operation in 1965. The Rockpile was a strategically important feature located 15 miles west of Cam Lo. The pilot of this UH-34 demonstrates the skill of many pilots in Vietnam who were regularly required to reach isolated groups of Marines. (NA)

Left: Members of the 7th Marines prepare to depart on an operation in 1965. Two of the Marines have World War II-era grenade carriers. Given its light khaki appearance, the man third from left appears, to be carrying one of his canteens in a World War II-era canteen cover. Also of interest is the helicopter pilot who is wearing a Vietnamese-manufactured tiger-stripe camouflage jacket. (NA)

Above: Marines rush to waiting helicopters. Each of these men has attached his entrenching tool to the back of his M1941 haversack. Reflecting lessons quickly learned since their arrival in Vietnam; each man has two canteens and a tropical first-aid kit attached to their M1961 rifle belt. (NA)

Right: Corps efforts to pacify portions of I Corps under its control was to interact with local Vietnamese civilians. Here, members of the 3rd Marine Division Drum and Bugle Corps entertain the residents of Dong Song One. The bandsmen are wearing OG 107 utilities that have been tailored to short sleeve length. Variations of ways to wear the utility cover can also be seen on each of these men. (U.S.M.C.)

Opposite page, top: Marines rush from their CH-46 helicopter during Operation Jackstay in March 1966. It was critically important to clear a landing zone as quickly as possible. These Marines are armed with the M14 rifle, which had replaced the venerable M1 Garand of World War II fame and had been in service since the end of the Korean War. (U.S.M.C.)

Opposite page, bottom: Men of the 5th Marines clear their landing zone during Operation Jackstay. To provide a less

conspicuous target, the large white MARINES painted on the side of the helicopter would eventually be repainted in black.

Above: A UH-34 gunner manning a door-mounted M60 MG keeps a watch on the ground below prior to dropping off Marines during an operation. The gunner is wearing Navy issue flying coveralls and a Nylon APH5 flight helmet. Both Marine and Army aviators used them throughout the war. (U.S.M.C.)

Opposite page, top: A scout dog team searches for enemy positions during Operation Macon. The Marines' distinctive M1941 suspenders and M1961 ammunition pouch can be seen on the man at left. Each pouch could carry one magazine for the M14 rifle, which this man is supporting on an improvised sling over his right shoulder. (U.S.M.C.)

Opposite page, bottom: Maj. Gen. Lewis W. Walt, the commander of the III Marine Amphibious Force (MAF) and the 3rd Marine Division, talks to his men at Qui Nhon. Walt is wearing the Marines' unique M1958 Cotton Sateen Utility uniform and black leather combat boots. Although the M1958 uniform was obsolete by the time the Corps deployed to Vietnam, older Marines wore it as a sign of stature. (NA)

Top right: Sniper Dalton Gunderson looks for enemy soldiers during Operation Virginia. Gunderson is armed with an M40. Later in the War, XM21's were fitted out with Redfleld scopes, and became the Marines' standard sniper rifle. (NA)

Right: Members of the 4th Marines search abandoned enemy positions in the demilitarized zone (DMZ) during an operation in May 1967. The man at the left is using a pair of M1941 Marine suspenders to support his combat load. (U.S.M.C.)

Men of the 12th Marines shell enemy positions from a 105mm howitzer in the DMZ during October 1967. Wet weather has caused the man in the center to wear a wet-weather Navy issue parka. Wet weather clothing such as this would be issued on an 'as needed' basis and would not normally be kept by a Marine. All three of the men wear their flak jackets. (U.S.M.C.)

Right: Two men fire their 81mm mortar at enemy positions near Con Thien in October 1967. Both are wearing Army OG 107 utility uniforms and World War II-era Marine rain caps. (U.S.M.C.)

Below: Despite enemy shelling, two Marines at Con Thien try and get some rest. The empty box between the two men is the case for boxes of C-Ration meals. After being given individual meals, Marines would remove the cans from the boxes (seen here strewn throughout the trench) take what they thought they could carry, and discard the rest. (U.S.M.C.)

Left: A Marine moves through a destroyed Vietnamese village during Operation Napoleon/Saline. Barely visible on his left hip is the case for the M17 Chemical-Biological Field Mask. Although poison gas was not used in Vietnam, the M17 was occasionally used during smoke attacks and the case was handy to carry additional belongings. (NA)

Below: Marines move into a destroyed Vietnamese village. The man at the right has attached his canteen to the eyelets located along the bottom of the M1955 flak vest rather than attaching it to the belt as was normally done. (NA)

Right: Marines move against an enemy position during Operation Napoleon/Saline. These men are equipped with M16 rifles, which began to reach Marines in 1967. The two men in the foreground are travelling light; extra ammunition for their Ml6s is being carried in disposable cotton bandoleers. (NA)

Below: A Marine prepares to search a building in Quang Tn Province. He has fixed his M7 Bayonet to his M16. Although infrequently used in close combat, bayonets could come in handy in poking through any belongings found in buildings or to intimidate a nearby enemy. (NA)

Left: Marines fire an M60 while the rest of the squad advances. The gunner has his issue .45-caliber pistol on his right hip in a black leather M1916 holster. He has also begun to personalize his helmet cover with a variety of graffiti. (NA)

Below: A line of Marines crosses an open area with their Ml6s at the ready. The Marine moving forward second from the right has been able to obtain an Army issue M1-C Airborne helmet liner (identified by the distinctive chin cup) for his MT helmet. (NA)

Above: Members of the 3rd Marines rest during operation Saline. They are all wearing green T-shirts with their tropical combat uniform trousers. When the first Marines were deployed to Vietnam they were forced to dye their issue white T-shirts themselves. Later arrivals received T-shirts that had already been dyed a green color. (NA)

Left: A Marine waits for the order to continue advancing during Operation Napoleon/Saline. He has been able to obtain two Army issue one-quart plastic canteens, with their distinctive top, to replace his issue canteens. Army plastic canteens were generally favored over the Marines' metal canteens, which would get hotter in the intense heat of Vietnam. (NA)

Below: A C-130 takes off from Phu Bai while Marines wait to be transported to the battle during Operation Chinook II. Two of the Marines in the foreground are wearing Navy foul-weather gear underneath their flak jackets. All of these men have attached two canteens and a tropical first-aid kit to the back of their M1961 rifle belt. (NA)

Left: Using issue nylon sandbags and empty wooden ammunition chests, two men work to build a bunker. Both are supporting their trousers with the Marines' distinctive Khaki web belt; army waist belts were made of black cotton webbing. The Marine on the right has attached his K-bar fighting knife to his belt. The World War II-era K-bar was still popular with Marines in Vietnam. (NA)

Below: Members of the 4th Marines move back toward the Cua Viet River at the end of an operation. Even though their mission is complete, these men still take precautions and leapfrog slowly back to their positions. (NA)

Above: L. Cpl. Joseph Ortiz (left) and L. Cpl. Robert Moore look for enemy targets during Operation Scotland II. Although they are both wearing earlier olive-green uniforms, both are wearing ERDL camouflage boonie hats. These camouflage hats became available to Marines in 1969.They were not so disparaged in the Marines as they were in the Army units. (NA)

Right: Lt. Col. Edison Miller (second from left), formerly a prisoner of the North Vietnamese, is interviewed by a marine movie team. All of the marines are wearing forest-green service caps and trousers with a khaki short-sleeve shirt. The forest-green uniform was not normally seen being worn in Vietnam. (NA)

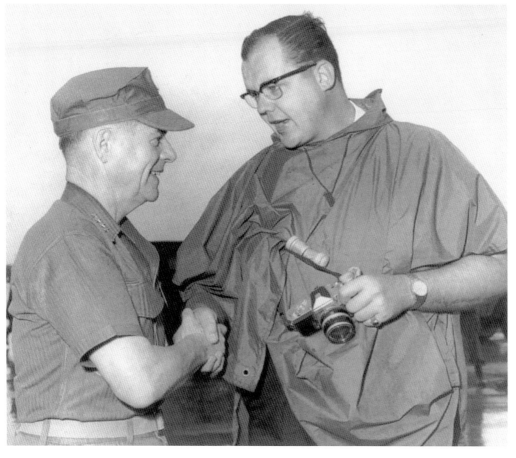

Left: General Wallace M. Greene (left), the commandant of the Marine Corps, discusses the military situation with Bob Gassauley, a war correspondent with the Associated Press. Greene is wearing the herringbone twill (HBT) M1956 utility uniform. Although widely used by Marines during World War II and Korea, by the time of the Vietnam War, the Corps had discontinued the use of HBT uniforms. (NA)

Lower left: Legendary correspondent Walter Cronkite (centre) interviews some men in Vietnam. The soldier being interviewed is wearing an Army issue M1952 flak vest. The Marine by the jeep is wearing a pair of locally manufactured tiger-stripe camouflage trousers with a standard olive-green jacket. (NA)

Right: L. Cpl. Greg Penta fires a .50-caliber machinegun at Communist positions around Khe Sanh. The 126-pound World War II-era .50-caliber machinegun was too heavy for ordinary use and was generally only seen at fixed positions and on vehicles. (NA)

Right: Marines at Khe Sanh work to improve their positions. The proximity of the enemy requires that they wear their flak jackets and helmets. Nevertheless, the man seated at center appears to be wearing civilian shoes with his Army-issue black socks. (U.S.M.C.)

Left: A Marine runs for cover during the brutal house-to-house fighting at Hue. In his left hand he is carrying a 66mm M72 Light Assault Weapon (LAW). The LAW was a hand-held, disposable, rocket that was ideal for the close in fighting at Hue. Draped around his left shoulder is the carrying bag for the claymore mine. These bags were a handy way of carrying additional equipment. (NA)

Below left: A Marine is helping evacuate a Vietnamese child from the ruins of her home. Rather than blouse his trousers with the drawstring found at the bottom of each leg, he has instead opted to simply roll up his trouser legs around the tops of his boots, which allowed for greater air circulation (NA).

Below: Two Marines raise the Stars and Stripes over a building in Hue. Although generally too warm to be used in Vietnam, the man on the left is wearing the M65 Cotton Sateen field coat. The expandable cargo pockets on the tropical combat uniform can also be clearly seen on the man at left. (NA)

Above: A Marine rushes past an M-48 tank during the fighting Hue. To improve circulation the running Marine has chosen to forego wearing a T-shirt under his flak vest. (U.S.M.C.)

Right: A Marine M60 gunner fires on an enemy position. Unusually, this Marine has improvised a black helmet cover, probably out of some sort of locally obtained material. A cardboard box carrying an additional 100 rounds of belted ammunition for his gun is just to his right. (U.S.M.C.)

Above: Marines with M17 gas masks prepare to charge into an enemy-occupied building. Use of masks was often necessary when smoke was used to clear buildings. The squad's radio operator (RTO) waits outside. His AN/PRC-25 radio is visible on his back.

Left: A Marine fires his 5.56mm M16 during the fighting for Hue while a comrade looks on. The M16 began to replace the M14 among Marines beginning in 1967. Although not initially as popular as the M14, Marines soon came to appreciate the weapon's lighter weight and rapid rate of fire. (U.S.M.C.)

Above: An exhausted Ontos crewman rests on the front glacis of his vehicle during a lull in the fighting. His M16 rests nearby on spare tracks for his vehicle. The Marines' method of blousing their trousers over the top of their jungle boots can clearly be seen in this picture. (NA)

Right: A Marine fires his M79 'blooper' grenade launcher at an enemy position while his friends look on. The man in the center has painted some sort of phrase onto the cover for his Ml helmet in white. While decorating helmet covers was not unusual, it was usually done in black. (NA)

Left: A Marine prepares to raise "Old Glory" over his position. The gusseted cuffs of the tropical utility uniform can be clearly seen in the picture. Also of interest is his long hair and full moustache. While such styles would not normally be allowed, under combat conditions regulations regarding hair were often relaxed. (NA)

Below: Members of Company F, 1st Marines, search for an elusive enemy near Route 9 outside of Khe Sanh. The Marine second from the right is supporting his equipment with a pair of Army issue M1956 suspenders. He is carrying clips for his M16 in Army issue M1956 universal small-arms pouches. Unlike the Marine's M1961 pouch, each Army pouch could carry multiple magazines. The use of Army equipment by Marines was very common as the war progressed. (U.S.M.C.)

Right: Two members of the 26th Marines fire an M60 on retreating Vietnamese soldiers in March 1968. Although usually fired using a bipod, the M60 could be used on a tripod, as pictured here. The use of the tripod would steady the gun and make it easier for the gunner to concentrate on his target. The Marine on the left has obtained a mesh helmet net that he has secured over his cover. The M1 helmet was generally only worn with the helmet cover. (U.S.M.C.)

Below: Two Marines work to string razor wire around their positions at Khe Sanh. Razor wire was regularly strung around fixed Marine positions throughout the war. The Marine working at right has secured an ace of spades underneath the rubber band around his helmet. Use of such personal talismans was a not uncommon occurrence as the war progressed. (U.S.M.C.)

Right: Two Marines fire a 105mm howitzer at North Vietnamese positions surrounding Khe Sanh. The World War II-vintage 105 mm served in a variety of capacities during the war. In the hands of a good crew the gun could deliver up to eight rounds per minute at enemy targets. (U.S.M.C.)

Below: Two Marines scan enemy positions from atop a bunker at Khe Sanh. The Marine on the right has stuck a K-Bar knife into his waist belt. First issued during World War II, the K-Bar was immensely popular with Marines and, since it was exclusive to the Corps, was worn as a mark of pride and distinction. This particular knife, with its light brown scabbard, would appear to be of World War II vintage. Vietna-vintage K-Bar knifes were issued in black leather scabbards. (U.S.M.C.)

Opposite page, bottom: Members of the 3rd Marines move into defensive positions after being landed near the DMZ in July 1968. As was common among both Army and Marine personnel in Vietnam, the man kneeling at center has draped an issue towel around his neck to wipe sweat from his face. Also of interest is what appears to be a plastic water gun stuck into the retention band of the Marine kneeling on the left. (NA)

Opposite page, top: From left, Corp. Gary Miller, L.Cpl. David Sullivan and Corp. Gail Culp of the 4th Marines race for cover at the start of an enemy attack on their positions at Cam Lo in 1968. The three men appear to have been going through boxes of C-rations (which are open around them) prior to the attack. Miller is reaching for his flak vest. (NA)

Opposite page, bottom: An M60 Team fire on enemy positions during fighting at Hue. The gunner at the right has chosen to wear his Ml helmet backward. Both men have 100-round belts of ammunition for the gun draped over their shoulders. For added protection, the gunner is wearing a .45-caliber pistol in a M191 1 pistol secured to his right hip. (U.S.M.C.)

Right: A Marine fires his M-79 grenade launcher at an enemy sniper during the fighting for Hue. Rather than carry rounds for his M-79 loose or in bandoleers, this man has chosen to modify a jungle jacket with two rows of individual pockets. Although unauthorized, such modifications were not uncommon. He has also secured an additional round for his grenade launcher underneath his helmet's rubber retention band. (U.S.M.C.)

Below: A Marine ANPRC-10 radio team waits for the completion of an air strike to be completed before continuing forward during Operation Auburn in July 1968. The ANPRC- 10 was eventually replaced by the lighter, and more effective, ANPRC-25 radio, which had a range of 3.5 miles. This radio operator seems to be coordinating the attack of the aircraft visible in the background. (U.S.M.C.)

Left: Sgt. H. D. Hines fires his M-79 grenade launcher into a suspected Viet Cong position. The 6.2-lb M-79 could fire five to seven 40mm grenade rounds per minute out to 430 yards and was a light indirect fire weapon that proved effective in dense terrain. (U.S.M.C.)

Right: A Marine officer radios in a report during the fighting for Hue. He has clipped an M26A1 fragmentation grenade to one of his equipment straps. He is carrying a pair of binoculars in a leather case on his left hip. Underneath his flak vest he is wearing a Navy issue wet-weather parka. The Marine to his left has been able to obtain an Ml-C airborne helmet liner, with its web chin cup, for his Ml helmet. (NA)

Left: Two Marines take cover from enemy fire during Operation Saline II. As was common, each of these men is carrying two Army issue one-quart plastic canteens. They are also wearing the tropical first-aid kit between their canteens (NA).

Below: Two Marines wearing M17 protective masks while waiting for smoke to clear from a suspected enemy position. The Marine in the foreground has fixed his M7 bayonet to his M16 rifle. He has also attached his rifle's XM3 bipod. Although it was light, easy to attach and could steady the rifle, particularly when fired in full automatic, the bipod was rarely seen being used in the field. (NA)

Below: A Marine gun crew manhandles their gun through difficult terrain. Rather than wear helmets, several of the men are wearing the Marines distinctive cotton sateen utility cap, which had first been introduced during World War II. (NA)

Above: Marines move through Hue after the fight for the city had ended. The Marine with his back to the camera at left is wearing a field jacket over his jungle fatigue uniform and flak jacket. The Marine walking second from the left has slipped another magazine for his M16 into the patch pocket on the front of his flak jacket. He has also clipped an M26A1 fragmentation grenade to his vest. (U.S.M.C.)

Below: A Marine M-48 tank supports advancing infantrymen during the fighting for Hue. The large square box at the base of the tank's 90mm gun is a Xenon searchlight, which could be used to blind an opponent and light up a battlefield. Spare water is carried in World War II-era 'jerry' cans stowed on the back of the tank. (NA)

Right: A tank commander watches infantrymen advance. The commander has draped a towel over his shoulder to wipe sweat from his face. He is holding his left hand up to the helmet's internal communication system. Unlike the World War II-era tanker's helmet, the Vietnam-era combat vehicle crewman's helmet offered some ballistic protection to its wearer. Note the field-modified pintle for the .50-calibre MG atop the cupola, which provided a greater arc of fire while exposing the commander to fire. (U.S.M.C.)

Right: Elements of the 7th Marines move through dense jungle terrain during a search and destroy mission in April 1969. Rather than carry ammunition in the Marine's M1961 ammunition pouch or the Army's M1956 pouch, several of these men carry additional ammunition in disposable rifle bandoleers. Each bandoleer could carry up to seven clips for the M16. (U.S.M.C.)

Above: Members of the 26th Marines are taken off Hill 5 by a CH-46 helicopter during Operation Oklahoma Hills in April 1969. The majority of these men are all wearing the ERDL camouflage pattern jungle utility uniform, which began to be received by the majority of the Marines beginning in late 1968. Also of interest is the variety of Army and Marine issue web equipment being worn by the men. (U.S.M.C.).

Opposite page: Marines load a round into their M-107 self-propelled 175mm gun. Each round for the M-107 weighed 150lb and could reach targets up to 20 miles away. The M-107 was the heaviest piece of artillery used by the Marines in Vietnam. (U.S.M.C.)

Right: Two members of a Force Logistics Command rifle company search for enemy positions near Da Nang. The Marine at the rear is carrying a M1941 Marine Corps rucksack but is supporting his combat load with Army issue M1 956 suspenders. His helmet is draped off the back of his rucksack revealing the helmet's web suspension system.

Above: A Marine Landing Vehicle Tracked Personnel (LVTP-5) approaches Barrier Island Beach during Operation Daring Rebel in May 1969. Often referred to as an Amtrac (amphibian tractor), the LVTP-5 could transport as many as 34 combat ready Marines into a battle area. The vehicle was ideal for use in Vietnam's numerous waterways. (U.S. Navy)

Below: Members of the 7th Marines display some enemy bicycles that they discovered during an operation in the Que Son mountains in November 1969. Three of the men are wearing issue boonie hats in the ERDL camouflage pattern. Reflecting conditions in the field, these men all have haircuts that are a far cry from the 'high and tight' usually pictured on Marines. (U.S.M.C.)

Right: An M60 machine gunner and his assistant fire into a building suspected of holding an enemy sniper during Operation Oklahoma. The assistant on the left is carrying three Army issue plastic canteens on his belt, which is supported by M1956 suspenders. He is also wearing an 'in country' manufactured boonie hat. These privately purchased hats often would have a more rigid form to them so that the brim could also be snapped up on the side. (U.S.M.C.)

Below: Members of the 4th Marines cling to the sides of an M-48 tank travelling down a road near Con Thien in January 1969. Unlike the tanks' crewmen, all of the passengers are wearing their flak jackets. (U.S.M.C.)

Left: Lt. Wesley L. Fox from Leesburg, Virginia, catches up on hometown news during a break in operation Dewey Canyon. Lt. Fox's rank insignia has been pinned to the left collar of his utility jacket. Use of insignia in combat conditions was often frowned upon because it would provide a target for enemy snipers. At his feet are several empty C-ration cans, which were the principal field rations used during the Vietnam War. Fox would receive the Medal of Honor for his actions on February 22, 1969, during a bunker-clearing operation. (NA)

Top right: Two Marines carry 120-mm artillery ammunition through positions in the Ashau Valley. The Marine at the front has draped a Charge, Assembly, Demolitions Bag M-183 over his shoulder. Like the Army's claymore bag, the demolition bag was often used to carry additional personal items. He also has a World War 11/Korean-era helmet cover in 'Duck Hunter' pattern camouflage.

Right: Marines inspect captured enemy weapons during Operation Dewey Canyon. The Marine standing at center is carrying an M1911A1.45-caliber pistol in a shoulder holster. Rather than wear a Marine flak jacket, this man has been able to obtain an Army issue M69 flak jacket, which offered its wearer greater neck protection (NA).

Above: Some members of the 9th Marines inspect captured enemy weapons during Dewey Canyon. These Marines have removed their flak jacket, which provides a good view of the Tropical Combat Uniform, better known as the jungle uniform. The uniform was constructed first in lightweight cotton poplin and later cotton 'rip stop' material and has been inspired by the World War II-era M1942 parachutist uniform. (NA)

Left: Members of the 9th Marines move into an abandoned enemy camp during Operation Dewey Canyon. The man at the rear of the column is carrying his folding M43 entrenching tool in its carrier while the man to his front has simply slid his through his equipment straps. (NA)

Above: A U.S. Marine (left) shows a South Vietnamese Marine how to set an M1 8A1 anti-personnel (APERS) claymore mine. The lightweight claymore was ideal for use in defending a position and springing ambushes on unsuspected enemy soldiers. When electronically detonated, the claymore would shoot 700 tiny steel balls out to a range of 54 yards. (NA)

Right: Marine helicopter crewmen smile for the camera at their base on Marble Mountain. The two men in the foreground are wearing Marine Corps issue CS-FRP-l coveralls in flying, summer, fire-resistant polyamide. The coveralls are light green and made of fire-resistant Nomex material. A Velcro patch on the right breast of the coverall allowed placement of a leather nameplate. The man on the right has stenciled his T-shirt with a personalized emblem. (*Vietnam* Magazine)

Left: Weary members of the 5th Marines cross open country during a sweep of Go-Noi island south of Da Nang. As was common with Marines in the field, the men of this patrol have chosen to wear T-shirts underneath their flak jackets and to discard their jungle jackets. The M60 gunner is using a towel to wipe sweat from his brow and to provide some padding to support the weight of the gun. (U.S.M.C.)

Below: Sergeant Michael Larkins (left) and 2nd Lieutenant Louis Daugherty display a tiger that tried unsuccessfully to get into their positions near Da Nang. Both men wear Army issue M1956 Load Carrying Equipment (LCE) over their camouflage jungle uniforms. Daugherty has taped his K-bar knife to his equipment suspenders. He has also stuck green electrical tape to his rifle to serve as camouflage. (U.S.M.C.)

Right: Private First Class (PFC) Kyle Pruitt prepares to test fire an M-2 .50-caliber machinegun. The World War-II-era .50 caliber was often mounted on vehicles to provide additional firepower. Although it could deliver a terrific 40 rounds a minute on enemy targets, its 126 pounds made it too heavy to be used by infantrymen. A metal can carrying additional linked rounds of ammunition for the gun is mounted in a cradle to the left of the gun. (U.S.M.C.)

Below: PFC Ruben William (left) and PFC Larry Mock, a two-man sniper team, look for enemy targets during an operation in January 1970. William wears an earlier olive drab pattern of jungle fatigues while Mock wears the newer camouflage utilities. Although it was largely obsolete by this point in the war, William continues to carry the M14 rifle, which the Marines had been using when they first arrived in Vietnam in 1965. Mock, on the other hand, uses an M40 sniper rifle against his target. (NA)

Opposite page, top: Members of a Marine Civil Action Program (CAP) team help a Navy corpsman administer a shot to a Vietnamese villager's cow. The utility cap of the Marine at the right has retained some of its shape. Usually, the heat in Vietnam would quickly cause the utility caps to lose their shape. All the men are wearing the camouflage utility uniform. (U.S.M.C.)

Opposite page, bottom: Two Marines wait for an air strike to neutralize a North Vietnamese position outside Lai An before moving up. The Marine at left is wearing a gray fatigue sweatshirt underneath his flak jacket. Both men have decorated their helmet covers with a variety of mottoes and stencils. Personalization of helmets, particularly later in the war, was common among both Army and Marine personnel. (NA)

Right: A Marine inspects a captured enemy machine gun. He has stuck a white plastic spoon from a C-ration box into the left chest pocket of his flak vest. Each C-ration contained one of these spoons. This handy implement was often retained in vests and helmet bands. (NA)

Left: Marines armed with M14 rifles rest along the side of the road during a patrol in 1965. They are all wearing the earlier 0G107 sateen utility uniform. All their jackets have been modified by having the sleeves shortened. The Marine in the foreground has obtained an Army issue M1952 flak jacket. (US Navy)

Below: Marines cover their ears as the M-48 they are riding on fires on enemy positions. The man standing in the center has a 66mm M72 Light Assault Anti-Tank Weapon (LAAW) draped over his shoulder. This one-shot, disposable weapon was frequently used against enemy fortifications. Rather than blouse their trousers over the top of their boots, the two men seated at the right have simply rolled up their trouser legs. (NA)

Above: An M2A1 flamethrower operator clears a path through thick terrain. The 42.5-lb flamethrower could throw a jet of flame out to a distance of 49 yards. Although heavy and vulnerable, the M2 could be very effective against enemy fortifications and tunnel complexes. (NA)

Right: An M60 gunner fires on a suspected enemy sniper position. This gunner has decorated his helmet with graffiti. One of the ammunition belt's disintegrating links rests on the top of the sandbag in the foreground next to the spent round. (NA)

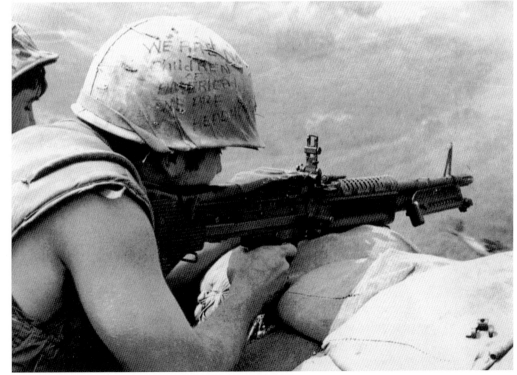

Opposite page: Members of the 4th Marines board a waiting boat near the village of Dai Do in Quang Tn Province. These men present a standard appearance for Marine riflemen during an amphibious operation. For longer missions, these men would also be carrying packs and additional equipment. (NA)

Above left: PFC Robert Ikner displays ordnance taken from a North Vietnamese sapper unit that attempted to attack his position. Ikner is wearing a privately purchased identity bracelet on his right arm. He also appears to be wearing the earlier version of the cotton sateen utility jacket with the sleeves cut off. (NA)

Above right: Members of C Battery, 13th Marines, fire their 105-mm Howitzer from Fire Support Base (FSB) Rattlesnake. The versatile 105 could be transported by helicopter to remote FSBs and provide much needed artillery support to Marines operating in hostile territory. This gun is being fired from the plywood pallet on which a helicopter delivered it to the FSB. Its position has been strengthened by using empty ammunition crates. This photograph was taken at the moment of full-recoil, hence the truncated appearance of the gun-tube. (NA)

Right: Maj. Stephen Pless sits for an official portrait after being awarded the Medal of Honor. Pless is wearing the officer's version of the Dress Bluejacket. The officer's version was in dark blue and lacked the red piping of the enlisted version. The Marines' EGA (Eagle, Globe and Anchor) insignia are visible on the collars of Pless's jacket underneath the ribbon for his Medal of Honor. The U.S.N./U.S.M.C. pilot's wings appear below the South Vietnamese jump-wings. (NA)

Left: Private R. Jones from the 7th Marines takes a break from carrying a mortar base plate. Jones has fixes his M6 bayonet to his M16. He is wearing wet-weather gear underneath his flak jacket and has been able to obtain an Army issue Ml C airborne helmet liner for his Ml helmet. His helmet cover is in the earlier, World War II-era duck hunter camouflage. Additional equipment is strapped to a plywood pack board at his feet. (NA)

Below: Maj. Gen. Lewis Walt, the commander of the III Marine Amphibious Force, visits his troops during an operation in 1966. Walt, standing center, has affixed a bronze EGA insignia to the front of his Ml helmet. Such additions to the helmet were more common in World War II and Korea than in Vietnam. The officer pointing to the right of Walt is wearing the 1st model jungle jacket and trousers with exposed buttons on the pockets. (U.S.M.C.)

Right: A 60mm mortar team supports an attack. The 45-lb '60' was lightweight and could reach ranges of 2000 yards was an ideal weapon for Marine units operating away from the reach of larger-caliber artillery units. Rounds for the mortar were carried in cardboard tubes, which lay at the feet of the gunner setting the bipod.

Below: A six-man helix team rush toward their waiting UH-34 helicopter at the end of a mission. Unusually, only the Marine at the front of the column appears to be wearing his flak jacket, while the others are going without. The Marine running second from the right is also carrying a collapsible M20 rocket launcher. The bulky World War II-era M20 would eventually be replaced by lighter weapons such as the disposable LAAW. (U.S.M.C.)

Left: A Marine fires his M16Al, with its birdcage flash suppressor, on enemy positions during the fighting for Hue. Underneath his flak jacket this man is wearing an M65 field jacket. It was usually too warm in Vietnam for the use of the heavier field jacket but occasionally, as at Hue, it could be seen in use. (U.S.M.C.)

Right: A Marine stands watch. The M16 is fitted with the earlier three-prong flash suppressor. The later M16Al had the 'bird cage' flash suppressor. He is wearing an ERDL pattern camouflage boonie hat, to which he has given a distinctive shape in order to personalize it. (U.S.M.C.)

Below: Maj. John Tyler (left) and Maj. Robert Miller of Marine Attack Squadron 314 examine damage to Tyler's F-4B Phantom at the conclusion of a mission in January 1967. Tyler wears the CS-FRP-1 coveralls, while Miller continues to wear the older Navy issue flight suit. Both of these suits could be adjusted by Velcro tabs at the waist. (NA)

Opposite page, top: Lt. Col. Eddie Pearcy looks on as Lce. Cpl. Howard Rice arms a bomb prior to a mission. During a 22-day period in March 1966, Pearcy and Rice's VMFA 542 dropped a record number of bombs and rockets on North Vietnamese positions. Pearcy is wearing a Navy issue flight suit and helmet, while Rice wears the army 0G107 utility uniform. The Marine's distinctive two-inch khaki web waist belt is visible on Rice. (NA)

Opposite page, bottom: Marines from the shipboard detachment of Marines on USS Hancock escort South Vietnamese pilots to a collection point on board ship after their escape from Saigon during Operation Frequent Wind. The Marine on the right has the Marine's distinctive EGA insignia stenciled to the left pocket of his shirt. These Marines are also wearing web pistol belts with a brass EGA plate. This plate was normally reserved for more formal occasions. (NA)

Above: An EA6A Intruder refueling in front of VMCJ-l revetments between missions. The pilot has camouflaged his flight helmet. Although initially issued in white, many pilots would personally decorate their helmets and eventually these were issued in more subdued colors. (NA)

Right: So many people were brought to waiting U.S. rescue ships during Operation Frequent Wind that helicopters had to be pushed off the decks of many of the ships. Here, a South Vietnamese CH-47 is pushed off the deck of USS Hancock. (NA)

Below: Marines from Company F, 2nd Battalion, 4th Marines rush toward CH-53 helicopters waiting on a soccer field in the embassy compound during Operation Frequent Wind. These Marines had formed a security perimeter while the embassy staff was evacuated. They are all wearing 0G107 utility uniforms with their M1961 load carrying equipment. (NA)